Mind and Blood

John Finlay, 1968 (age 27)

Mind and Blood

The Collected Poems
of
John Finlay

Edited by David Middleton

John Daniel & Company ❧ Santa Barbara, California ❧ 1992

ACKNOWLEDGMENTS

This edition of the collected poems of John Finlay includes poems
that appeared in the following chapbooks: *The Wide Porch and Other
Poems* (R.L. Barth Press, 1984); *Between the Gulfs* (Barth, 1986); *The Salt
of Exposure* (The Cummington Press, 1988); and *A Prayer to the Father*
(Blue Heron Press, 1992).

Some of the poems in this edition also appeared in the following
publications: *The Classical Outlook* Journal of the American Classical
League; *Drastic Measures; The Epigrammatist; The Hudson Review; Nine
Years After* (ed. Bob Barth, R.L. Barth Press, 1989); *Order in Variety:
Essays and Poems in Honor of Donald E. Stanford* (ed. R.W. Crump,
University of Delaware Press, 1991, courtesy of Associated University
Presses); *PN Review; Poetry Pilot; Samuel Johnson: Sixteen Latin Poems
Translated by Various Hands* (Barth, 1987); *Sequoia*; and *The Southern
Review*.

Library of Congress Cataloging-in-Publication Data

Finlay, John.

Mind and blood: the collected poems of John Finlay / John Finlay

p. cm.

ISBN 0-936784-99-7

PS3556.I486A17   1992

811'.54—dc20   92-8290

CIP

To Jean Finlay

In light apart from me, I seek the Word
Holding mind and blood from the absurd.

CONTENTS

PREFACE

JOHN MARTIN FINLAY was born in his maternal grandmother's house in Ozark, Alabama, on 24 January 1941. His parents, Tom Coston Finlay and Jean Sorrell Finlay, owned a peanut and dairy farm outside the nearby town of Enterprise, and there John Finlay spent his early youth coming to know firsthand the mystery, the beauty, and the hardship of agricultural life. He also became a deep and avid reader, sometimes reciting passages of Shakespeare to the cows (whom he named after Greek goddesses) as he took them to and from the pasture every day. After finishing public school in Enterprise, Finlay earned his B.A. (1964) and M.A. (1966) in English at the University of Alabama at Tuscaloosa and taught for four years at the University of Montevallo. Then, in 1970, Finlay entered the doctoral program at Louisiana State University in order to study under Donald Stanford, editor of *The Southern Review* and former student of Yvor Winters. Along with Allen Tate, Winters was one of Finlay's primary models of the poet-critic that he himself aspired to be.

Except for the years 1972-73, which he spent on the Greek island of Corfu and in Paris, Finlay was at LSU throughout the 1970s. He received the Ph.D. in December, 1980, after completing his dissertation on Yvor Winters' intellectual theism. (He also joined the Roman Catholic Church in 1980.) In 1981, Finlay left Baton Rouge for the family farm in Alabama where for ten years he wrote essays and new poems. On 17 February 1991, John Finlay died of AIDS, leaving behind his as yet unpublished book of essays on the Gnostic spirit in modern literature—*Flaubert in Egypt and Other Essays*—and three published chapbooks of poems as well as unpublished and uncollected poems, three essays from an unfinished book on the

Greeks, and several diaries kept in Enterprise, on Corfu, in Paris, and in Baton Rouge.

Finlay's poems are almost all in traditional literary forms. He mainly wrote plain-style lyrics of direct statement, short narratives, or else post-symbolist poems whose sensuous details exhibit controlled associationism in which definite ideas and feelings are indirectly yet logically presented. Whether plain-style, narrative, or post-symbolist, Finlay's poems are serious, simple, deep, direct, and often traumatically revealing of the human condition. The best of them are truly unforgettable. Finlay addresses such subjects as the origin of the mind, the relation of mind and matter, mind and the irrational, mind and God, the nature of evil, Thomistic theology, philosophical subjectivism, the inscrutability and beauty of the natural world, primitive religious rituals, and, especially in the later poems, family life in the South since the early nineteenth century, Indian life in the South, the nature of modern war, and the isolation of the serious thinker and artist in the contemporary world.

Particularly impressive are poems in which these themes are confronted by one or another of Finlay's heroes of the mind including Odysseus, Oedipus, Solon, the exiled Ovid, a Benedictine monk, Samuel Johnson, Audubon, Henry James, or Sherlock Holmes and poems in which characters such as Narcissus, Spanish gold-hunters, Descartes, and Rimbaud suffer various forms of self-delusion which warp or destroy their moral nature. Among Finlay's most poignant and tragic figures are those who, through madness or disease, allow us to see beyond their suffering and unawareness the divinely ordained, objective moral grounding of the world. Examples of such characters are the mad women in "The Locked Wards," the shattered Confederate veteran in "The Blood of Shiloh," and the hate-filled, natural-law-denying novelist in "A Portrait of a Modern Artist."

Among John Finlay's papers (now at LSU) is a remarkable prose statement written to accompany an (unsuccessful) application to a foundation for financial assistance to provide the poet time to research and write a long narrative poem on Audubon. In this statement, which amounts to a poetic credo, Finlay says: "I do not intend for [the poem] to be a loose, vaguely subjective account of this cunning, single-minded Frenchman. I hope that it will be rooted in history and fact, and evolve from actual observation of Audubon's wilderness, or the little that is left of it today. This does not mean that it will be unpoetic. For me the greatest poetry comes, not from fantasy, but from intense, realistic perceptions of the natural and human worlds." Finlay goes on to discuss the central idea of the proposed poem: "The theme is the immersion of Audubon's mind and art in the American wilderness of the 19th century, his recovery from it, and then the discipline and passion necessary to understand the experience and translate its beauty into art. Audubon is the prototype of the artist, who has to shift back and forth between two sometimes conflicting worlds: the experience of the wilderness, immediate, sensual, non-intellectual, and the mental state of detachment from that experience, in which the mind works through the wilderness into art."

Finlay never wrote this longer poem, but he did write a fine shorter poem on Audubon. A late paragraph in Finlay's statement is related to this poem: "the last part will be much the longest and broadest in scope. Here [Audubon] realizes his art and makes his first really significant breakthrough....We see him in his semi-intuitive, semi-intellectual contact with the raw, even primitive aspects of the wilderness, and observe the cunning and craft he used to get his prey and then to reproduce the almost inexplicable mystery of its livingness, the actual look in the mockingbird's eye as it hovers in the air, poised, its wings outspread, ready to fight the rattlesnake coiled tightly around its nest." This mysterious struggle of the artist to do justice to the objective world is captured in the final lines of the completed poem "Audubon at Oakley":

> I saw my book, taut wings of mockingbirds
> In combat with the snake knotted beneath
> The nest, its open mouth close to the eggs,
> Now held forever in the lean, hard line.
> And underneath, defining them, combined:
> The clean abstraction of their Latin names,
> The vulgate richness of this Saxon salt.

Now held forever in the lean, hard line. Readers who want serious poems that vividly present sensuous experience as understood by a mature mind steeped in classical and Christian tradition, yet fully aware of the problems of the contemporary world and of the perpetual threat of the primitive and the irrational, should find much to their liking in *Mind and Blood*. In their severe and uncompromising grandeur, John Finlay's best poems are surely permanent additions to American literature.

—David Middleton

Note: This edition of John Finlay's poems bears the title and the epigraph Finlay himself chose for such a collection. Late revisions Finlay made in 1988 to some of his earlier poems are incorporated here. The poems in Section IV were found among Finlay's papers after his death: these poems were composed between the mid-1960s and the spring of 1990. Except for "At Some Bar on Laguna Beach, Florida, Winter, 1969" the uncollected poems in Section V were all published during the 1980s. (See "John Finlay: A Bibliography, 1971-1991" in *A Garland for John Finlay*, David Middleton, ed., Blue Heron Press, Thibodaux, Louisiana, 1990).

Mind and Blood

I. The Wide Porch and Other Poems
(1984)

THE WIDE PORCH

For M. C. F.

Where nothing can be other than it was,
I hold the house as solid in my mind
As it had been before it was destroyed.
Standing in sycamore, live-oak and pine,
Still the seasons soak its holding frame.

Susanquas blooming in the winter sun,
Air cool inside like water from a well
As summers peeled the painted walls outside,
Fall rains sounding in the rooms all night—
These laved and filled the backward mind.

I see our family on the wide porch,
In sun that thickens to a wilderness—
The upper columns seethed in summer bees—
And know the past encoded in the blood
As deaths perfected it and sealed it up.

I swept away the clotted leaves and dirt
From graves my uncle took me out to clean.
The massive autumns drunk in their own seed,
Staining the chilled slabs, nothing underneath—
I then moved outward to become myself.

She who last lived there, finally alone,
Died terrified, flesh holding on to flesh.
No cries came when that agony had ceased.
We closed her eyes, transfixed in nothingness,
Then left her covered in the naked light.

I left the house. The sun was rising keen
In burning fog away from each bright leaf.
A swimmer coming out of blinding salt,
I stared where trees stood rooted in a world
Brutal and calming in the clearing sun.

AT CLAYBANK

Your parents lie buried
Under emblems of waves.
Cold surges of granite
Secure the ancient graves.

After pain and blindness,
With clouds closing in,
Summer lightning and rain,
We bring you to your kin.

What you asked is done.
You lie in their pure flood.
The rain washes the clay
Above it, dark as blood.

IN THE ADRIATIC

In translucent night, rising from the sea,
The coastal mountains ended in the moon.
Up to their heights, cultivated groves
Held them in place. Under reflecting leaves,
The turning undersides of thin pale fish,
The twisted olive trunks were rooted deep.
Miles down, in isolated clefts of rock,
As in a well, black water sucked the base.

A FEW THINGS FOR THEMSELVES

Along the bay live-oaks and magnolias
Gather massively the warm blackness
As birds dart and cry in their hard leaves.

At their base the narrow strip of beach
Is yellow and African in the late sun.
We hold off and let the boat drift....

The string of fish in the bottom
Lies in spilled oil, blood and bay-water.
Their white underbellies gleam in the dusk.

A black watersnake is moving into
The closed, muscle-like blooms of lilies,
The darker swamp weeds along the shore.

Slowly we follow it, back to the dock.
And walk in the early night through crickets,
The low wind in the rusty screens.

THE LAST ACT

'Tis the god Hercules whom Antony
Loved now leaves him.

It is too often only close to death,
Or utter failure, when the mind is held
To truth, we see the outlines of the gods,
Those whom we loved but never realized.
Above us in a void burnt-out and cold,
At unfamiliar heights their forms return
Like ghosts to move across the final night,
Remote and unappeased in our collapse.
There is no bitterness in facing them.
The heart that fatally kept them deprived,
And saw them hostile to the living blood,
Will pay in blood its error, every vein.
In what is not the gods are reconfirmed,
The candor of their presence briefly seen.
The tragedy leaves nothing else but that.
Then they are gone. The music underground,
The quiet terror of its shifting source,
Its echoes vanishing, moves in their place.

ASH WEDNESDAY

The floor is cold on which I kneel. Unclaimed
As yet by any grace, I try my mind
On rottenness and sin revealed and named
By law, but hear within the loosening bind
Of flesh, instead, determined in its plight,
The spoiling heart irrelevant and tight.

THE BOG SACRIFICE

The iron and acid water of the bog,
Rising and falling with the winter rains,
Two thousand years, preserved him as he died,
Pinned naked to the floor by wooden crooks.
No fire had cut and cleaned the clotted soul.
Runic stakes, washed white as salt, were laid
Over his narrow breast, sunk in the peat.

The sacrificial rope they hanged him from,
Of woven skins, still cut into his throat,
Tight as when death came. His gentle face,
Forced upward by the torsion of the noose,
Bore with monstrous discipline his bane,
As loose ends, like serpents, meandered down
His naked length, pressed into his flesh.

A cap of wolfskin hived his shaven head.
Descended from a line of conscript priests,
He died in youth, still delicate and whole.
When he was lifted from the pit, the earth
Itself then sweating like an ancient beast,
He looked as if alive. Faint cries of snipes
Brought sunlight piercing to his closing eyes.

Before Christ reached this isolated north,
A chthonic goddess, holding iron breasts,
Each year in early spring exacted death.
In winter when the winds blew keen off ice,
Or summer with its rippling swarm of weeds,
The bog seemed never raised above the sea,
But underneath, out of whose depths she came.

NARCISSUS IN FIRE

He moved apart. For nights in solitude
He watched his mind, in anguish at itself,
Exhaust the will and, burning in its own
Locked speed, turn into itself, deprived
Of those objective forms sustaining life.
He saw the blackness breed another scheme,
Himself the landscape surfacing brute waste.
And stared into its moon until his eye,
An open pulse, beat in the rustic fire.

THE BLACK EARTH

In the beginning was a crime...
—*Hannah Arendt,* On Revolution

Toward dawn a dusty mirror frames the moon.
With lines cut on the surface of the glass,
I watch it rising like a fire in space.
The walls of my small room are burnt away.
Like prehistoric time the past floods up—
Fields rising in moonlight from solid oak,
Swamps where lidlessly the snake slid down
Gutted banks, pine-quiet, into the light.

The moon was god. Its white compulsive fire,
Reflected from the pits of scattered seas,
Transfixed the eye and cut the veinless core.
To keep from savage sleep, at nights I clung
To what one light left burning in the house
Saved of my room. I stayed above the dream,
Until the mental walls and floors dissolved
Against my will, and mind and light were lost.

I killed the father in the mangled dream,
A wasted man who strained his cruel life
Taut as barb-wire pulled on rigid posts.
His fields stood bearded under summer noons.
I dreamed instead the fall, the rotten wheat
Uncut, the sound of hawks in foreign skies,
The father found alive on the black earth,
The blindness made by me to hide the crime.

As punishment, the breaking mind absorbed
Into its very blood his bloodless ghost.
I woke in sweat. The open window framed
The steady light, the bare, distended skin
Of earth on fire outside the narrow room.
I fought to hear the scream I kept inside,
But still, a naked thing, I heard his voice
At once both curse and cry, condemning me.

The moon has risen white. The mirror clears
Of darker fire. His voice now fades like pain
A human takes, absorbs, and then survives.
This moon itself will fade, whose cobalt glow
The dawn soon strikes to almost nothingness.
Throughout morning it will but faintly gleam
There in the west, a disc of thin white bone,
The center eaten through with constant light.

THE FOURTH WATCH

...and about the fourth watch of the night he cometh
unto them, walking upon the sea....
—Mark, VI, 48

No fictive dawn discloses me some god,
The foam of rabid wolves, the guts of fish
Kept from his tomb not fixed in any sod,
Where nothing speaks whatever is his wish.
In light apart from me, I seek the Word
Holding mind and blood from the absurd.

At every move some bruised, malignant part
Of me, that evil I have not withstood,
But found instead within the viscid heart,
Resists the sequent meaning of the good.
A lightning screen of images stays time
To fix me in a wordless past still blind.

You made us out of nothing, primal Word.
Not lost or spilt in uncreated waste,
My essence is not You by matter blurred.
But nothing leaves in me its mortal taste.
I am because of You. And in Your claim
I find my life and speak Your holy name.

On earth You spoke to heal demonic men
Begging wholeness in the splitting tomb,
Who saw You out as God through utter sin.
The sea beyond the will, archaic spume,
Night's fourth watch below the human mind,
You also calmed and left to its own kind.

Embedded mind sustains the complex whole
Redeemed with blood of Deity made flesh—
You save the man, not disembodied soul.
And summer burns the tireless sun afresh:
A wedding-feast out under shade of limes,
The servants brimming water-jars with wine!

ODYSSEUS

In honor of Yvor Winters

I could not know the meaning of that time
I lay long nights upon those rotting planks
To hear the wind blow wild in shredded sails,
Until I heard the voyage beat out in words.
When the blind poet ceased, I went outside

And stared down slopes below encrusted walls
Whose stone absorbed the cries of closing surf.
From where I stood I saw, at its low edge,
The narrow beach that, momently submerged,
Withstood the wide explosions of the tide.

THE ARCHAIC ATHENA

Small owls in the spring nights
Whirr through pines below her shrine.

The new-skinned snake sleeps
Full-fed in its temple cage.

Her wooden statue washed in the sea
Gazes through foam of the moon.

Wisdom knows the grasping root
Ending as thinnest hair in waters

Held pure and trembling in a well.

AUDUBON AT OAKLEY*

My Gallic cunning poured sweet wine into
The calyxes of trumpet-vines and caught
Small drunken birds a bullet blows apart.
Others I shot, pinned them to a board
To draw the fresh-killed life. Elusively,
The *is* that quickens in the living eye
Escaped the sweat of art, drying ink.
I tore blind pages till I reached the one
That pleased my avid mind. The wilderness
There teems with birds I never saw before:
White and wood ibises, the sparrow hawk,
The red-cock woodpecker, and painted finch.
I hunted them for days and nights until
I throve in timelessness. One day stood out.
I heard below all things the river sough;
The fall was blazing in the silent trees.
I saw my book, taut wings of mockingbirds
In combat with the snake knotted beneath
The nest, its open mouth close to the eggs,
Now held forever in the lean, hard line.
And underneath, defining them, combined:
The clean abstraction of their Latin names,
The vulgate richness of this Saxon salt.

*Oakley was a plantation outside St. Francisville, Louisiana, where
Audubon lived and worked during the summer and fall of 1821.

Three Voices After the Greek

Archilochus

1. *Between battles*

Bring wine that has a bitter bite
And thickest oak to burn through night.
Forget the dead, the vultured tree,
The other deaths that soon must be.
My soul, stay firm through all of this.
My only strength is drunkenness.

2.

You dainty officer, poor muscle fool,
Keep flashing that unbloodied sword of yours
At these crude asses in this savage Thrace:
You'll finally get it stiff as any boor's.

*

Sappho

1.

What is most lovely? Some say cavalries
Of Asia, teaming chariots, or fleets,
Winds spreading sails in turgid strength.
But I say what one loves. How plain to see!

2.

Cool water ripples through the blooming
trees, this spring air, and falls
in ceaseless waves on my pliant flesh,
Goddess out of the spume on depths!

*

Callimachus

Don't come to me for bolts and thunder.
Zeus is the clerk for all that lumber.

Note: The first Sappho and the Callimachus are translations. The
others are original poems based on the material of each poet.

II. Between the Gulfs
(1986)

THE FIRST EMBLEMS

Veins of sea-
weed, thin
bones of fossil
fish, the print
of shells in stone
turned inward
to the core.
Gulleys choked
with kudzu.
Miles down
the bleached road,
the hot salt
and the white
Gulf at noon.

ORIGO MENTIS

I was the bastard, or the younger son,
The immigrant, suspicious and detached,
Who left the womb of crowded villages
For seas no rooted mother-god could cross,
And off barbaric coasts of Asia sought
My white star rising in the moonless heat.
Island cities of my breathless birth!

*

And yet no place explains my origin.
The tender, gut-like smoothness of inside
The brain a barrier of bone defends.
There I fuse with matter, human flesh,
And apprehend the essence and the thing.
If I am ruthless with most mysteries,
The knotted one I cannot solve is self.

*

One lightning bolt of abstract thought
Defined godhead so clearly that it left
The primal gods exhausted by the earth,
Enormous buttocks, faceless heads of sex,
The dying god, his seed at any cost.
It ended too the worship of the dead.
When what is deathless makes the argument,
Nothing mortal can survive its point.
I burned the body others kept and begged.

*

But nothing is forgot, an irony
That bitters me at times. Once conceived,
Its image lives in Hades of the mind,
The elegiac night of formless tombs
And speechless absence hot as brutal fact.
One drop of me though changes everything.

*

It was dense poems and Socratic light,
My endless afternoon before the war.
Shade of the plane made water underneath
So cool at noon, and in the summer too.
We waded in the stream and then lay back
Upon the sloping bank. Cicadas sang
Those monotones of music made with fire.

TWO POEMS FOR OEDIPUS

I.

You blind King Oedipus, emblem of mind,
In whom Apollo sunk those awful claws,
No fate forced you to learn your crimes.
The god left free kinetic intellect,
Deathless, matterless, itself like god,
Which cuts like acid to a final cause.
You chose and seized yourself the agony
Of kingship, goat-song of purest law.
Unshadowed noon, the isolated throne,
Clearing of marble lit by reason's god—
You held these blinded in your sacrifice.

II.

For all the oracle compelled you to,
You could have been some faun in Thebes,
Full of warm experience, and simply died.
You once saw in a barn at night an old
Bull's innocent eyes lifted to a lamp,
The buried roof above him sifting snow,
And felt a moment's kinship to the brute
As totally you drank his essence up,
Poseidon's bull, the sea as solid flesh!

IN ANOTHER COUNTRY

Untouched in his reserve and luminous,
The self I could have been yet never was,
Stared half-conscious of my being there.
Discovered in the autumn woods, he sat
In the dry grass, finished with the kill,
Resting for the final walk toward home.
A mess of dove and quail lay at his feet,
The rifle gleaming in the level sun.

As if he waited awkward for my other fate,
The mind abandoned then on open earth,
And knew the justice of its stranger life,
He moved, evading me, into the closing dark.
And, in his place, the other self awoke
In the fierce sunlight of a foreign room.

THE CASE OF HOLMES

The *scientific searcher* scans the blood,
The objects in the room, the tracks of mud,
Thickest around the pathos of the corpse.
He doesn't let instinctual grief that warps
The vision cause him not to find that fact
Which later hangs the murderer. Abstract
And lean, he seems emotionless cold thought,
Almost at times as sexless, always taut.
He has to drug a mind that will not cease
Once a case is solved—cocaine's release,
Or trance before the chemical blue flame.
And there are states of mind he cannot name,
As skulking in the fog, urban night-wood,
He feels compressed, erotic brotherhood
And for the hardest criminal. But these
Are freakish states and disappear. He sees
Himself as whole in this: revulsion for
The *great malignant brain* who wages war
On those who break an ego's brutal dream.
He matches brain to brain in the extreme
Of hot collected nerves and cold reserve.
Fear also makes him whole; he must preserve
One being in the conflict with that brain
Or else, at one mistake, he will be slain.

THE DEFENSE OF SOLON

Black earth, the mother of immortal gods,
Be my bond that what I speak is truth.
I pulled out of your sacred soil the stakes
Of land-enslaving predators and healed
Your wound back in the ancient families.
To Athens, citadel of light, I called
Back home those exiles sold in slavery,
Whose being was debased in foreign tongues.
I freed the Greeks oppressed by Greeks
And broke the rabid force of brutal men.
I never was afraid of power. I fused
It with strict justice, disregarding blood,
And made a rod I used to rule the state.
Justice bade me pay homage to the whole.
The sun-struck body gleaming in its sweat,
Its health confirmed in agony of games,
But body lit with light of ruling mind—
That image formed my model for the laws.
And yet I had no peace. The broken parts
Of faction begged me ceaselessly to force
Myself as ruthless tyrant on the state
So they could live off me like parasites.
I knew that solitude in tyrants' souls,
Their only friends the thugs of bodyguards,
Their only life a dream of purest fear
Disguised as arrogance and endless greed.
I fought them off and held tenaciously
The juster mean excluding mad extremes
And in the end I was reviled by everyone.
But yet I cannot think that I have failed
Though Athens chose the tyrants after me.
I wrote the laws on everlasting stone.
I did not leave them on the heart or trust
Their substance to the memories of men.
They will survive my private death in time
And Athens' slavery now proves their truth.

THE INFERNO OF THE AMERICAS

We floated by islands never seen
By human eyes. Perfume of their trees
Stunned the sense in the wild sun.

Sudden transparencies disclosed
The ocean's depths—we hung beguiled,
Like gods drunk on this universe.

At night we saw the stars, myths
Of the old houses, burn up and flake
In phosphor on the lunar sea.

The green and white tree-boas,
With two lungs and vestiges of claws,
Choked the upper trunks of ceibas

Under which on land we moved
And found the gold of naked Adam,
White bones in eternal heat.

THE JUDAS TREES

I saw she had come back from hell itself—
Sweat clung to her delicate white face
Whose fine bones haunted me as a small boy.
Her voice again I heard in the dry air,
Gentle yet precise as her ironic brain:
"How can you live through your absurdity,
Religious pain? Hell at least is pure."
Scorn still ate the vitals of her soul;
A sexless tenderness burned in her eyes.
"I heard for weeks my brother beg to die.
I felt his pain. I hated God that night
I killed a living corpse to give him peace."
She lived alone and kept ferocious dogs;
She read her Virgil and the Civil War—
The seed of Troy in the young Confederates
Killed by Yankee Greeks, the women sold
As barren slaves to a vulgar modern fate.
But in her lonely mind that murdered God
She was just as modern as all the rest.
The last time I saw her alive she looked
Defined in death. Protected by her dogs,
She showed me an old garden she still kept,
The judas trees blooming beside the wall,
Buds of quince among the gleaming thorns.
She nearly stumbled, blinded in the sun,
The vernal light reflected from the soil,
But held her balance as I reached for her.
"Do not touch me if I do fall," she said.
"These dogs of mine will eat you up alive."

A ROOM FOR A STILL LIFE

Delicate stalks meander through blue silk
Rootlessly and float blooms white as milk
Upon the sofa's green. The polished floor
Reflects the island of the room the more
Pelagic light pours through a wall of glass.
Some books of images are stacked *en masse*
Beside an open clock. Light thickens now;
The colors change; a copper gold somehow
Like acid etches things, an unseen knife,
The cliffs of vividness, mortal still life.
The modish woman lifts her head to face
The god across the room. A circle base
Supports his damaged body; rods connect
His shattered thighs; each part is flecked
With minute stain. But yet the pieces hold,
Become themselves pure art, imagined mold,
In her acute though cool aesthetic mind.
It is the fragment, something not defined
But felt through nerves outside the whole,
Which satisfies and gives her mind its sole
And isolated act these days. Time seems
The kind of autumn light one sees in dreams,
Which floods a fictive object she had made,
Which floods her too against a wider shade.

DEATH IN ASIA MINOR

At a Coastal Shrine in the 2nd Century A.D.

Indigo feathers of the slaughtered cocks,
Against white marble, blacken in the chill
Late afternoon. A priest will burn them soon
Within the precincts of this god who dies.
The bowls, the whetted sacrificial knives,
Already washed of blood, gleam in the studs
With sunlight failing in the circled shrine.
The bearded image, with the dog and snake,
Stares lidless at the columned yard outside
Where frost is thickening on the bare ground.
Water brims, nervously is poised in pools
Fed by the springs erupting underneath.
Below the cliff, the winter sea cries out,
The shrine invaded by the constant sound
Which mounts into the quiet brain to make
In them at night, entranced within the god,
Low undertows of noise.
                              The men extreme
Who stay all night, have purified themselves,
In thinnest water cleansed demonic flesh.
They lie, some with knives, on narrow beds,
Locked inside a room sealed off from light,
Sifting dissolving fragments of the brain
To find this distant god who comes in blind
Destruction of the mind. Each strains to be
The shipless winter sea, or timeless fire
That eats itself alive, the human knot
Dissolved or burnt, in water or in fire.

The oldest dreams again he hears the wind,
Crying in frozen trees, before the dawn,
When he had stared abstracted at the tide—
The whole wave pulled to pieces by the moon—
Then bled himself, according to the dream
Wherein the god had spoken through the wind.
As he awakes, though blind as when he slept,
The thawing sun, which smokes itself into
A frozen world, lies cindered in his mind.
He stands on ice and sees the nervous threads
Of blood, again, unskeining from the gash.
The dawn repeats the sea, now leveled flat,
Solid in livid blue, like trembling slag,
The broken banks, the cries of preying gulls.
The rind of self now burning in the god,
Nothing reclaims his gutted mind, a skull
Soon cleaned, the body drained, cast in a grave
To break and darken, costing him no pain.

AT KERKERA

Erosive waves cut knives
Spining this spur of rock.
Above, walled strata lock
A shrine in solid hives.

No one can go inside
Its jutting room to see
The Christ in agony
Or know His end alive.

We live below His death.
He waits for us enshrined.
The dark iconic mind
Feeds on mortal breath.

TO A FRIEND ON HIS FIRST BOOK

How strange seeing your poems in a book....
I once could feel the pathos of those nights
About them still in hottest Baton Rouge,
Black coffee, poverty, the sweated line!
They only are themselves in this rich book.
I read them as a stranger, not a friend—
Poems get deathless, out of our control—
And see the man who started them consumed.

Two Epigrams

I. *The Hunter*

What I kill my folk live on for life.
What I slay I must respect to prove
My skill and stoic calm in deadly strife.
I get the wound in what cold seasons move.

II. *A Fragment for the Fall*

In the slanting gap of night black crickets
Keep at their song on the lean earth and frost.
All night a full moon burns the bare thickets,
The skin of earth, the river blind and lost.

THE DEAD AND THE SEASON

To my uncle killed in a farming accident during the Fifties

The western sides of barns stay oven-hot
Where insects glue the tight cocoon of eggs—
Air blowing off the Gulf, the pouring sun!
Fire has cleaned off stubble from the fields;
What once was yours lies fallow in the light.
Late autumn afternoons your mother dreams
That you come back. *How can it ever change?*,
She asks out in the dusk of settled gold,
The dead, the season fused inside her soul.

But change will come. Under the iron sky
The winter oats will grow on frozen earth.
This dawn we pulled a heifer's early calf—
One leg bent backwards clogged the passageway.
We cleared its nostrils of the viscous film
So it could breathe. The mother's afterbirth
And broken blood lay steaming in the chill.

Why am I telling you this?, you dead
These many years and surely now indifferent,
Or arrogant, to things involving blood.
In one full night you paid the mortal debt
On sheets soaked through, then never changed.
Why would you now come back? We ourselves
Deserted you. We shunned for rawest guilt
What seemed pure evil in your bloodless face
So that your end was strangers and a priest.
We lived the remnant of that morning blurred:
The chilled and silent house, engulfing light,
Some neighbors who had come to cook our meal,
The slugs of scalding whiskey for our blood.

THE ROAD TO THE GULF

A small white town, its silver water-tank
Gleaming above a green deep river's bank,
We passed before the pastures still unmowed
And melons piled for sale beside the road.
Samples were cut on shells of oyster blue,
So ripe the seedless heart had split in two.
The closer to the Gulf we came the more
The flattened earth recalled itself as shore.
The needle of the pine, metallic leaf,
Grew where lusher life would come to grief.
The soil lay dreaming of the ancient salt,
A trance of heat inside the summer's vault.
It cooled by evening when we reached the bay.
Black vistas opened out; just miles away,
We felt the plunging shelves of rising sea.
The boats were in; at shore beneath a tree
The scaling boys half-naked, brown as nuts,
Threw to the blue crabs the fishes' guts.

III. The Salt of Exposure
(1988)

UNDER THE REIGN OF THE ACTOR

Cocaine and money cure and fix our wills.
He makes us little gods for other ills.

OVID IN EXILE

The frigid Bear-star ranges near the place
Where now I try to live among a savage race.
My exile lies north of the crucial straits
That flow between my Europe and those gates
Of Asia, north where the edges of the world
Fall off in bearding ice and hang uncurled.
The unmapped inlets of the fierce Black Sea
Wash through my open prison. I live free
Where Roman grace has never drawn the soul
Or taught its basest motions self-control.
Winter lets down the upper hordes who cross
The frozen Ister that, liquid, was a fosse.
Witches made poisons for their arrow-tips.
Death-hunger goads them on and Mars equips
Their shrunken minds with fury for the kill.
After they leave, these villages stay still
For hours; survivors then emerge from holes
And cremate murdered kin on oak and coals.
It is the white, void endlessness of snow
That seals the mind inside, and fungi grow
Within its darkened core. My Roman life,
My poems' fame and friends, my absent wife,
All seem absurd, unreal. I strain in tears
To focus on their forms. Among my fears,
The chief is of their death in my own mind.
To keep my Latin pure and still enshrined,
Like someone crazed, I talk out loud alone.
I but half learn the gutteral harsh groan,
The snarl of spit they use as human speech.
They think the poet queer, a woman-screech
Who froths beneath the madness of the moon,
Who best is simply killed off in her swoon.
I hide my poems from these vulgar tribes.

And still I write—my muse alone inscribes
Some peace, some reason on my lonely rage.
I then am steeled to finish through my age.
If Caesar should forbid me still my home,
My death lies here. My poems live in Rome.

FOR HENRY JAMES

You stared at, as you died,
the warships on the Thames,
gigantic blank hulks
of steel bound to a war
blinded to your distinctions—
your last discovery of Europe.

How far away they seemed,
the great summer houses....
Against the richest light
on old lichened walls,
all through those afternoons,
limpid, suffused with gold,
the endless talk went on.

And afterwards, in the pools
of candlelight, among
cut-flowers in huge vases,
the tall French windows
closed against the night,
not one gesture betrayed
your own beast of deprivation,
waiting in the scented air,
eluding even you.

How private you became...
with nothing left at the end—
no Europe or America—
but stoic courtesy,
death a *distinguished thing*.

DESCARTES IN HOLLAND

He did not care to understand one word
The burghers said, and let thick fog create
A whiteness rendering his eyes absurd—
He had his mind inside for purer fate.

TO A VICTIM OF AIDS

Nurses who come near you wear masks,
As if your flesh breathed fatal germs.
They act absorbed by routine tasks,
As if there were, for them, no terms
For what it's now your eyes that ask.

The dark back rooms you sucked cock in,
The prolonged sweat of "river-rats,"
Of what you called "tight city-skin"—
The dudes, the studs, the alley-cats—
Destroyed the man that you had been.

You scorned judgement—pure tyranny,
You said, of some cold, proud elite—
Yet were the slave as you set free
The lord of flies, who swarms the meat
Of self-despair, your sex in debris.

Your body became your state of soul.
It can't condemn one thing, but must
Permit what comes, with no control.
The germ not killed now breeds in lust
On its own self, and kills the whole.

A ROOM IN HELL

In this tinted half-light
The snake scar of error
Is blurred; careful insight
Intoxicates itself.

The surf of phantasies,
Drenching deathless mind,
Dissolves rigidities,
The little we had been.

Outside, the soul's sleet
Whispers the warp of ice.
Further out, waves beat
Themselves apart and cry.

AT A SPANISH FORT
NEAR THE PENSACOLA NAVAL STATION

Black cannons of this coastal fort
Lie silent now. The mouth of fire
Is filled with vines; bees make report
In powdered blooms which they desire.

The fort had stood three centuries
Guarding the entrance to the bay.
Vain in our pure war's totalities,
It falls to myth and thick decay.

Our warriors are freed from earth,
Angelic, clean, new minds which hate
Those limits of our mundane birth,
Which soar outside the mesh of fate.

We hardly see the whitening jet
Straining toward the blinding sun.
Our mind can only sense its threat
In sound, its screaming loaded run.

ON THE VIETNAM WAR MEMORIAL

The dead's full names are cut
On depthlessness of glass—
The long war's human glut
On naked walls in grass.

They cut slab in bare fact,
Like graves without a cross.
Their art could not abstract
One meaning from the loss.

DUNESCAPE WITH A GREEK SHRINE

The further dunes receive the pounding sea.
>They never stay the same—
>Both wind and wave constrain
Their shapeless drifts so they can never be.

They are the graves of trash washed up by the sea,
>The whitened battlefield
>Where moon and ocean yield,
But leave their symbols in the stunted tree.

We wait until winds clear the moon and see
>The burning oil inside
>A shrine above the tide,
Protected by these dunes out of this sea.

AFTER SAMUEL JOHNSON'S LATIN POEM
TO THOMAS LAWRENCE, M.D.

By your life, then, will you confess
Yourself with crude mobs who attack
The wise, who call their power a fake—
Loud braggart fleeing in distress,
Whose only wounds disgrace his back?

You live through evils none ensures
His life against, from which we find
The holy and the brave do not escape.
You have the skill of potent cures,
But miss those purges of your mind.

Throughout the tediousness of night,
Blind opened depths for anything,
Throughout the unworked hours of day,
Cares blot out your paternal sight
And to your core distraction bring.

More than enough of grief at length
Is paid. Raise yourself up from gloom.
You hold the means and know the way.
The healing art, dead sages' strength
Demand from you their life and room.

Sacrifice some human things to God.
Let faith be grace to the tough truss
Of steel men have—do not inveigh.
You bleed on strangest ground unshod.
Come home to your strong mind and us.

AFTER SAMUEL JOHNSON'S *SUMME PATER*

Father most strong, whatever You intend
As to my body's fate—but Jesus, plead—
Do not destroy my mind. Can I offend
In begging life in me for Your own seed?

THE BLOOD OF SHILOH

My father came home from the War too weak
To purge its taint. My brother, a young man,
Survived like some hard thoughtless animal
And never grasped our father's broken mind.
My mother, too, though yet a faithful wife,
Eyed him in ignorance, but hers had scorn—
How could a helpless man work out our life?
Her soul as hardened as her callused hands,
She had turned bitter stoic through the War,
Working to save a threatened farm to keep
The children of her womb from being starved.
For life she killed the woman in her soul.
My father turned to me. At first I thought,
A doting daughter, rest would cure his mind.
Days he seemed himself, but they were brief.
Some fever of the brain seemed stuck in him
That grew in strength when he resisted it,
Some force of slaughter that his gentleness
Never could approve. He strained to fight
It off at night; he could not sleep but kept
One lamp beside his bed, staring for hours
Into its wick, moths thudding on hot glass,
As if he craved to be that piece of cloth
That stayed itself and never flaked in fire.
Only at dawn would sweating sleep dissolve
The demon in his mind, would he have peace.
It was the blood of Shiloh, he once cried,
The waters of Snake Creek that poisoned him.
Wounded in what is called the Hornets' Nest,
A gullied road clotted with Northern guns,
He lay that night out in the storming rains.
Lightning revealed the bodies of the dead,
Their open mouths vomiting out white rain.
And in a sleet at dawn he heard the screams
Of men whose limbs corpsmen were sawing off.

His whole mind broke, its warm interiors
Held by the corpses splattered in the sleet.
The God whom he had loved, a perfect good,
Did not survive that slaughterhouse in him.
Reason and faith bled out his inner core.
Only an ingrained discipline, though weak,
Forced him, rote-like, to finish out the war.
It then was worn out. Madness settled in,
And to escape, he came back home and died.
Our body's frame will not bear long a pain
Lodged in the mind—death will seem release.
I prayed for that, out of my love for him.
I feel God's mercy found his godless mind.
He went mad not because a coarsened brain
In him craved evil, for he craved the good
Whose absence his good mind could not endure.

A MEMORY OF THE FRONTIER

Cold wilderness outside, the burning lamp
Beside the bed whereon the old man died
I still can see back of the crowded years,
His white beard yellow in the oily flame.
That winter froze the river; the dogtrot
Whistled in the wind, and still he held
Us in his dying's vise. He broke at last.
The old slave woman who had lived with him
Cleaned the body laid on cooling-boards.
It made me shiver glimpsing water poured
On flesh in that cold time. The women-kin
Tore his bed apart. They took the sheets
Outside and burnt them in the evening fog—
Fire struggled on the clamminess of blood.
The men had had the coffin done by dark.
The neighbors came; huddled at the hearth,
We held a wake, then buried him by noon.

THE HISTORY OF A TRADITIONALIST

He learned what tougher masters can impart,
The salt and muscle of that English art
Before crazed adolescents wrecked its mind.
He took the meat out of the antique rind
And never aped mere manners from the past.
He never fetished tight control. At last
He found the style for plainest naked truth
And in some wisdom bore the end of youth.

And what was his reward in all the lights
Of magazines, rock-stars, and Reaganites,
Of liberal cant about the good, safe id
That only needs the State to screw its lid?
We cannot even say he had one rotten lot.
They absolutely treated him as he was not.

A PRAYER TO THE PARACLETE

God the Spirit, inspire
Our soul's and body's life
With purifying fire.
Let not quick sin be rife.

Cleanse the barren mind
Of crudities and lies
That it, at last, may find
Truth which fructifies.

Let charity fuse whole
The fractured, wounded will,
Each movement of the soul
To God Who makes us still.

And never let despair
Defeat the Father's plan:
Christ gives us God to share
In His shed blood as man.

ON REMBRANDT'S PORTRAIT OF AN OLD MAN READING THE SCRIPTURES

Exposure salted his grave Northern face.
An unerasable sadness tinged that grace
Of sourceless light glowing on solid form.
Hard winter nights—the isolating storm—
His oil burned out onto the living word.
A man matured in loss, in griefs incurred
By love outside himself, he would expend
His mind on God, still opened to the end.

THE AUTOBIOGRAPHY OF A BENEDICTINE

I teach logic to would-be priests,
The subtlest training of the Schools.
A keen, well-bred old hound unleasht,
I track down fallacies of fools.

I read dry Horace, drink wine deep,
Though never yet to drown my wits.
Old Cock is cooked, and so I sleep
The long nights unshaken by his fits.

I feel at ease here on this earth
And love the dogma of God's flesh.
Why should we see a poisonous dearth
In what God still creates afresh?

That sun-struck Porch of Solomon,
Those eunuchs of the maddening groan
Who insult reason, who would stun
Our souls with God, I leave alone.

Athena's grove, its tempered air,
The autumn sun on her olive trees—
I thrive and bead my thankful prayer
To reason's source for clarities.

Our mind is not some Virgil cursed
To go back down to painful shades.
Faith dies itself and is dispersed
In minds the deathless Word pervades.

A PASTORAL OF THE PRIMITIVES

By early June the limbs of the pear tree
Already sag. The weight of its thick fruit
Snaps its joints in just a random breeze,
So rich the womb of meat around the seed!
Sunflowers thrive and blow in deep manure
Where we had kept and fed the fatter bulls
We killed and ate. Noontide is like a god
Who pours himself into the teeming plant
So that we see its essence in white heat.
Only the gross catfish in coffin-vaults
The cows drink water in escape his fire—
They float full-fed on algae and rich scum.
The afternoon expands; the air stays hot.
A bush-hog chews across the pasture just
Below the house, splattered in iron-weed.
White egrets swarm for insects in its wake.
The cows stay for that cooler later time
Before they graze, then eat into the night.
They only stop to throw the head of tongue
Over their backs to kill the biting flies,
Leaving coats of spittle on their hides.
Our sight cannot detect the twilight's end
Or night's degrees. Earth fades in black
Extending upwards from the sunken swamp.
Bullfrogs in sexual heat cry desperately
As a full red moon is rising in the east.

SALT FROM THE WINTER SEA

My great-grandmother said each year the men
Would travel to the Gulf—a hundred miles—
To draw salt from the winter sea. They camped
Beside their wagons in the wild sea-oats
And built up fires of lighter-knots and pine.
Black pots boiled for days among the gulls
Upon white dunes, sea-water steaming off
And leaving salt. They sifted out the gross
Impurities. In cool depths of hogsheads
The fusing salt was stored away from heat.
They worked the surf like primitives afraid
Of gulfs, who never sought the sea herself,
Who lived inland and knew the solid earth.
But the last day, after their work was done,
Those stoics lingered in the cloudless calm,
The warm November sun of their Deep South,
The green Gulf crashing on the golden sand.
They momently then gazed outside themselves,
Struck by the mortal beauty of the waves,
Before they packed the salt and started home.

IV. A Prayer to the Father
(1992)

GO LITTLE BOOK

Go little book to the party,
But hide your moral crumb.
Be cunning. Act as if to say,
I'm hungry, Sir, and dumb.

A PRAYER TO THE FATHER

Death is not far from me. At times I crave
The peace I think that it will bring. Be brave,
I tell myself, for soon your pain will cease.
But terror still obtains when our long lease
On life ends at last. Body and soul,
Which fused together should make up one whole,
Suffer deprived as they are wrenched apart.
O God of love and power, hold still my heart
When death, that ancient, awful fact appears;
Preserve my mind from all deranging fears,
And let me offer up my reason free
And where I thought, there see Thee perfectly.

—Spring, 1990

THE FAUN

Est-ce en ces nuits sans fonds que tu dors et t'exiles?
—*Rimbaud,* Le Bateau ivre

He could not sleep. For hours in solitude
He watched his mind in terror at itself
Exhaust his will and burning in its own
Locked speed close in upon itself to dredge
The half-forgotten wreckage of its depths.
The buried images that it tore through
Loosened in the brain's imagined light
As in an atmosphere whose cobalt glare,
Unblinking and cold, absorbed and distantly
Defined the lonely havoc of their drift:
Savannahs rolling in the threaded swarm
Of their own growth lay burning in the slow
Contagion of the sun; again through fog
He saw against their open fires at dusk
The narrow settlements from which he knew
Himself estranged; rejected forms appeared,
Their bodies still abandoned in those nights,
Of women he had forced or gulled into
The brief and awkward void of his lust;
The childhood face of his drowned brother,
Untouched in its reserve and luminous,
Stared helplessly at him as with no mind
Of any choice it sank and was dissolved
In waters held engulfing in his mind.
The gods! The slaughtered herds and images
Drenched in blood! He now saw in his loss
Their far-off purity. No blood nor agony
Compelled that cold archaic peace nor reached
Those distances. The warm unshadowed noons!
The slanting gaps of night!

                              Outside the cave
He glanced across the quiet waste that lay
In cold moonlight for miles below the ridge.
From where he stood he saw at its far edge
The narrow beach that momently undone
Withstood the wide explosions of the tide.
And in that noise he walked until the dawn.

AT KALÁMAI

Bones in cold weeds
are what the sea can know.
All night it waited
outside the house,
you beside me sleeping.
Towards dawn it turned.
The waves crashed
into the cobalt haze,
gave out unto the moon.
They never were enough.
What dream were you turning in
that what I kissed was salt,
lay silent in those sheets?

THE *ILLUMINATION* OF ARTHUR RIMBAUD

African sunlight seared the grimy walls,
The windows opened to the furnace noon.
He gazed into its objectless pure style,
Hermetic light destroying common earth,
Until he saw the fated animal reach night,
This century of holocaust and suicide.

BAUDELAIRE IN BELGIUM

A gradual snow that hides abandoned flesh,
Death engulfs me as the moments pass.
Exhausted mind is ended now, old nag,
For hope leaves it as cold as argument.
The gathering mass will give me in its thaw
A dark and broken thing that costs no pain.
And I? The hooves are bloody from the ride.

STONE AND FIRE

L'automne déjà.
—*Rimbaud,* Une Saison en Enfer

The wine is drunk more slowly now. It clears
The turgid mind, unbends the wrinkled palm.
Forget, it says, the shives, the rust and smears.
Come take stoic stone, kind colorless balm.

In the slanting gap of night low crickets
Keep at their song in the lean earth and frost.
All night a full moon burns the bare thickets,
The skin of earth, the rivers blind and lost.

FLAUBERT IN EGYPT

He was awakened, for no cause he knew,
To face the brutal moonlight in the room,
Burning the veinless marble of the floor,
Flooding the nameless whore who slept on it.

As if he dreamed, he saw her open mouth,
The painted coins, strung around her throat,
Turned colorless as chalk in the strong light,
The gleaming black skin of her milkless breasts.

He thought of the pearl-fishers diving down
To layered tons of pressure on the skull,
With only shells to answer for the pain—
They surface, bleeding from the eyes and ears.

He dreamed the poem, freed of human act,
A smooth blank thing that turns in nothingness.

A PORTRAIT OF A MODERN ARTIST

The taking years have left her here alone
Out in rough country miles from any town.
Always the victim of the deadly male,
She writes hard fiction, all belief now gone,
And faces fate in nothing but cold style.
She labors on one novel through the years,
A Flaubert fishing by obstinate isles—
With her backwaters of the modern South.
A house lit blue by TV screens at night
Where Man and Woman tear themselves apart
After *he had fucked out her female brains*
Is matter for her art, her *fleurs du mal.*
Her characters burn out on sex and drugs.
How clinical she stays, how unconcerned,
As if she would respond to nothing now
But brutal slang and filth that's purified
Of thought, a rotless plastic of the mind.
Why does she strain at trash, compulsively
Work tone and structure right for the insane,
And cut the moral tissue from her soul?
She craves cool surfaces of some black god,
Nietzsche's dry savagery immune to pain
And tests her strange endurance in her art.
With no recoil she sees there moral law
Annulled and dreams chaos come back again,
A world of sex and death shot up on coke.
But during sleep she finds clear limits of
Her tolerance for evil. Sweat breaks out
And her disowned humanity comes through.
Aroused then by the terror of her dreams,
Alone out in the country late at night,
She screams herself awake to stop the fangs
That would tear out her life. Instinctively
She holds to her own form and being's stuff
Against the now felt madness of her art.

THE LOCKED WARDS

Thick walls enclose these women in a tomb.
Blind windows mock the sun that never strikes
Their buried rooms. No season reaches them,
Old and insane, whom only death will find.

The wound will never close. The acid poured
Into their textured souls forever clings
And eats their minds each day. Convulsively,
The need to void the evil claws for life.

One stalks the corridors, clutching torn rags
Against her breast. The disintegrating eye
In the electric glare holds her dead child
Alive each night, whose image burns in sleep.

Jesus, the youngest cries, *You died for us.*
She turns to face them all, then offers blood
Cupped in her rigid palms. Expanding veins
Deny the senseless skull, the hopeless pain.

Inside their cells, the women who have killed
Assume or plead the dead who torture them
Chained to their iron beds. Only near dawn
Do drugs dissolve the brain in sweating sleep.

These walls dissolve. The soul will never be
Absurd, though flayed alive inside this pit.
The madness spawned by loss, the filth of crime
Reveal its naked essence filled with need.

"IF A MAN DRIVE OUT A DEMON..."

I know that evil is the absence of a good,
A mind deprived, a truth misunderstood,

A nothing that cannot exist apart
A host, a dark obsession of the heart.

I know, also, existence offers us
In all its forms a way to end the curse.

All this I know, but error follows me
Even to this white page. I live to see

These words, so capable of flesh, become
In me mere fops of concept, wanting scum.

THE END OF THE AFFAIR

I leave now your dank underground small room
Where your lonely cold ego meets its doom.

I lived there lacking objects feeding sense
And vital conflicts, strengthening if tense.

We tried to eat each other's flesh instead
To get at blood which would appease the dead

Who lived on still in us as tragic script.
My bitter reason baulked. It took and ript

My book's mad leaves—I had to turn from you
Conning your hieroglyphs that are not true.

EPIGRAMS AND BRIEFER LYRICS

My friend says epigrams have an easy wit.
He would prefer that twitching bit by bit
Conceit of what he's never sure is it.

*

All morning at work
The poet is one thought.
Flies crawl and copulate on
His motionless hand.

*

The benefit of enemies is this:
Identity, too loose and vague in bliss,
Is clenched into a tight emphatic fist.

*

FOR ALLEN TATE

If now our lean language can sing
Of laurel and the rough dogwood
Caught in the single glow of faith
That led the salty Aeneas to Rome,
It is because of Master Tate.

*

THE GESTAPO IN THE APARTMENT OF FREUD

What moral force could you command to face
Their brute intrusion in your private place?
Your id is speechless, does not know of death,
Obscured by blood inside its rabid breath.

EPIGRAMS FOR ADVENT

1.

To free us from the dust to dust He came
And made it ashes of the Phoenix flame.

2.

Be patient. The Silent Word unspoken
Moves in all this broken world unbroken.

*

SKIN-FLICKS

The air-conditioning grinding like a fiend
Out-noised the crying bodies on the screen.

THE PIONEERS

The white man aimed his rifle at the head
And waited as the chief approached the house,
Soundless on muffling needles of the pine.
A band of young braves moved behind his back.
They came emerging from those sunken woods
Where one clean spring erupted in a creek.
The white man fired exactly when the chief
Had reached a clearing in the pine and stood
Exposed, a target lit by shafts of light.
The chief fell down convulsive on the ground
And died; his band was struck with terror at
The gun; a panic seized them and they fled.
The whites remained inside the house all day
While buzzards scented in the air the rot
And closed in tighter circles on the corpse.
The night came on in fluid blacker depths,
A shell of hungry forest cats and wolves.
And when the dark was done the dawn revealed
The body of the chief was now just bones.

OFF HIGHWAY 27

Vines choked off the chimneys
Of the few houses left standing
In those rusted abandoned fields.
Frames froze into the earth.
As windowpanes caught the sun,
Insides burned distantly away.

THE SEASONS OF THE BLOOD

The bulls of deep summer
grazing in thick fields,
wading through gold light...
unslaughtered, still alive!

In the fall the old dog
dreams of the bloodied catch.
The winds of the hurricanes
beat against his brain.

These winter stars shine
in depths and nests
of nakedness. We sleep
the long night in blood.

The snake leaves its skin
in the breaking spring—
its wrinkled self nailed
into new earth by rain.

I WILL NOT LET THEE GO

After she fell and broke her hip she stayed
In her back room. Her more than ninety years
Completed her. The yellowed shades were drawn
To cause the coolest dark for her weak eyes.
Her face was indistinct; her flesh collapsed
In those long dewlaps hanging from her arms.
And yet her voice was clear, her words precise.
The massive structure of her bones remained
To make her seem still strong in her old age.
The skin had wasted from the swollen joints
Of her huge hands that hooked like eagle claws
The arms of her wheelchair as she would talk.
"My father cleared us land. That teeming womb
We worked until it gave us our full lives."
Weakness of brain attacked the outer shell
Of present time and killed its just born act.
It left intact her mind's deep core, the past
With sunken roots that only death could pull.

FOR DAVID DURING DARK TIMES

For my sole self, inside myself alone,
Close to a heart, the poem's humid source,
Between a nothingness and pure event,
I wait the echo from my breadth within,
That cistern bitter, grave, and resonant,
Soul's vibrant mold, forever possible!

—from the French of Paul Valéry

V. Uncollected Poems

AT SOME BAR ON LAGUNA BEACH, FLORIDA
WINTER, 1969

Outside a night of sleet
That whispers the warp of ice
And low waves that repeat
What always is said again.

Inside a tinted half-light
Blurred the scars of error.
Careful, suspicious insight
Lost its edginess.

Moral strenuousness
Was disarmed by accident
Casual as the hit or miss
Of balls on green baize.

And a defenseless vacancy
Declined into obscurity,
Its thin margin a fantasy
Of surf that shivered onto ice.

THE GRAVES BY THE SEA

A translation of Paul Valéry's Le Cimetière marin

This tranquil vault, assuming files of doves,
Is quivering between the pines and tombs.
The perfect noon composes there with fires
The sea, the sea, the always rebegun!
After abstracting thought, what recompense
In this long gazing on the calm of gods!

Sacred travail of purest lights consumes
The many diamonds in the sightless foam,
And massive peace bethinks itself alive.
When one sun trusts itself above the void,
The pure effectings of a deathless cause,
Time scintillates, and wisdom is the dream.

The constant hoard, Athena's simple shrine,
Calmness of strength, and visible reserve,
The prideful depths, Eye holding in yourself
So rich a sleep beneath your veils of fire,
Oh my own silence!...Building in the soul,
The vault a thousand tiles, heavy with gold!

Temple of time, my essence found in breath,
I climb and use myself to this pure point,
Engulfed inside my vision of the sea.
And for that sovereign gift I owe the gods,
The calm explosion of this light now seeds
A regal scorn in staring down on heights.

Just as fruit melts in our possessing it,
Changing its absence to deliciousness
Inside a mouth in which its form will die,
So here I scent the fumes from my own pyre,
And to the soul consumed the sky intones
The rumors of these seething, changing shores.

That clearest sky observes me too in change.
After astringent pride, after so strange
An idleness, yet filled with pending power,
I now give up myself to burnished space;
Over houses of the dead my future shade
Subdues me to its own gaunt pace on graves.

The soul at solstice naked to its fires,
I am sustaining you, refulgent justice
Of light itself, your shafts so pitiless!
I cede you pure back to your primal place:
Regard yourself!...But to reflect the light
Requires that other part of dismal shade.

For my sole self, inside myself alone,
Close to a heart, the poem's humid source,
Between a nothingness and pure event,
I wait the echo from my breadth within,
That cistern bitter, grave, and resonant,
Soul's vibrant mold, forever possible!

Do you know, false prisoner of leaves,
Gulf devourer of these slender rails,
On my closed eyes, a secrecy that stuns,
What body drags me to its languid end,
What brow attracts it to a soil of bones?
A spark remembers there my absent ones.

Sacred and closed in bodiless pure fire,
A chthonic fragment sacrificed to light,
This fatal place is pleasing, held by suns,
Composed of gold, of stone, and sombre trees,
Where so much marble trembles over shades—
A faithful ocean sleeping on my tombs!

Shining bitch-hound, keep out idolaters!
When by myself, my peace a shepherd's smile,
I keep and graze the flock, mysterious
White sheep, of all my quiet tombs for hours,
Keep away from here the cautious doves,
The useless dreams, the busy, prying angels!

Once here, the future is an idleness.
Sharp insects cut across the brittleness;
Everything is burnt, destroyed, or shrunk
Into I know not what severe an essence....
Life must be vast, so drunk it is on absence,
And bitterness is sweet, the mind is pure.

The hidden dead fit firmly in this earth,
Which holds them warm to drain their mystery.
The Noon on heights immobile, absolute
There knows itself, agrees with self alone....
Complete pure head, and flawless diadem,
I am the secret, living change in you.

You only have my soul to hold your fears.
My guilt, uncertainties, my blind constraints,
These flaw the water of your perfect stone....
But in their darkness under marble slabs
A people vague among the roots of trees
Have slowly come to seize your primal side.

They have dissolved into thick nothingness.
Red clay drinks our own kind colorless—
Arteries of flowers absorb the given blood.
Where are the dead's unique, quick idioms,
Their arts of being selves, their only souls?
Worms work through where tears were formed.

The sharp cries of girls aroused and felt,
The eyes, the teeth, the eyelids fluid wet,
The maddening breast which teases with desire,
The blood which blazes in the yielding lips,
The final gifts, the fingers guarding them,
All goes to earth, falls back into the game.

And you, proud soul, do you expect some dream
Not stained by all these colors that deceive,
Which sea and gold make here for eyes of flesh?
Will you then sing when you are only air?
My presence now is porous—all must die;
Your sacred restlessness must cease and lie.

Gaunt immortality, gilt-lettered black,
Consolatrix fixed hideously with laurel,
Who transforms death into a mother's breast—
That pious ruse and myth too beautiful—
Who does not know, who yet cannot refuse
The stretched eternal grin, the empty skull.

Father in the depths, unhouseled heads,
Lying beneath that weight of spaded soil,
Who are the earth and who confute our steps,
The true gnawing, the irrefutable worm
Is not for you asleep beneath these slabs—
He lives off life—it's me he never quits!

Love, perhaps, or even hatred of the self?
His secret tooth forms such a part of me
That any name seems right—no matter what!
He sees, feels, dreams, desires and wills!
It is my flesh he likes; even in sleep
I lie transfixed by his unclosing eyes....

Zeno! Cruel Zeno, the Eleatic one!
You cut me with that arrow feathered taut,
Which quivering will fly but never move,
The sound begetting, arrow killing me!
Ah sun, a tortoise shadow for the soul,
Achilles motionless in breathless strides!

But no!...Arise! Into successive time!
My body, break apart this pensive mold;
My chest, inhale the naissance of the wind!
A coolness, rising off the breathing sea,
Gives back my soul....Ah salty potency!
Run into waves to re-emerge alive!

Yes! Giant sea endowed with ecstasies,
Hide of Bacchic panther, chlamys slit
By thousands of those icons of the sun,
Hydra absolute, drunk in your blue flesh,
Biting endlessly your glittering tail
In noise as deep as silence is its like,

The wind is rising!...We must try to live!
Immense air riffles through my taken book;
A reckless wave bursts pulverized on rock.
Let brilliant pages scatter in the flaws!
And crash, waves, crush this tranquil vault
Where crying taut sails plunged, predators!

THE EXILES

In honor of Janet Lewis

1.

The battle took place early fall between
The red men and the whites. But it was brief.
Before the unknown magic of the rifle,
The red men, panic-struck and terrified,
Collapsed and fell apart, and when their chief
Was shot, their power ebbed totally away.
The whole tribe then was rounded up; the old,
The women and the children, all of them,
Uprooted from their land and local god
Were herded west to eke out foreign life.

2.

Time passed, perhaps a week. One afternoon
I felt an eerie crawling on my skin
As when we sense someone unseen close by.
I was outside. I raised my eyes to see
An Indian woman standing in the yard,
Who had been separated from the tribe
And now was wandering in search of it.
A child hung from her back in woven straw.
Her sudden presence startled me; she seemed
Uncanny till I saw she was of flesh.
Warm sunlight cast her shadow on the ground.
She didn't make one sound, but cupped a hand
And raised it to her mouth. I went inside
And brought back food for her, along with milk.
She slowly ate and drank to make them last,
Then swung in front of her the strawed papoose,
And took her child and nursed him on her breast.
She rested there on our porch a little while
And left as silently as she had come.

113

3.

For some time on the woman lived in me;
I followed her inside my taken mind.
Those nights unsheltered and exposed, the bed
Of leaves on ground too damp and cold by dawn,
The long hard night, the two would have endured
So closely joined I thought of them as one.
I wondered if she found their tribe or if
She and her child were killed by animals or men
So that they lie unburied on wild earth.
The wolves and rattlesnakes she would have faced
Both on the open ground and in the woods.
But if the worst occurred, it was the life
I saw and felt, not death, which stayed with me.
And though some years have passed, I yet can feel
The sunlight of that afternoon in fall
When she consumed the food and fed her child.
I see the exiled pair, the woman's strong
And toughened face, the strangely silent child's
Leaning rearward from his mother's back,
Gazing toward the home he now will never have.

IN THE TIME OF THE CIVIL WAR

I

They were young immigrants, a man and wife,
Who had appeared one day the year before.
They farmed a lot outside our Deep South town
And lived alone but for my father's kindness.
Old men hanged him one morning before church
Out in those water oaks just north of town.
After they lashed the mule drawing the cart
On which he stood, the limb swung down too low
To let the rope cause death. The posse dug
Out with their hands a hole beneath his feet.
But even so, his feet dragged on the ground
As he swung to and fro. He never screamed
Or broke the Sabbath calm of the thick trees.
His unblindfolded eyes, abstract near death,
Were clear in pure despair behind the sweat.
He was their *foreigner*, his dark skin proof
He spied for Yankees, planted in our South.
And when they left their victim in the flies,
My father cut him down, then dug his grave.
We buried him that day. There were no kin.
The wife, who only spoke their native tongue,
Was near raw madness in my mother's charge.
When she regained her mind, my father took
Her to Mobile from which she sailed for Rome.
It was before the blockade sealed the South.

II

His dreaming mind detached him from the earth.
He lived abstract, as if some sterile knife
Had cut his soul from flesh so that it lived
Unfed with blood; still his eyes were vague,
Not focused on those men and things he saw,

115

But on some dream of them, in which he sliced
Them from their common nature, their own soil.
My father tried to save his soul; he talked
With him at length and liked the man in spite
Of his strange mind, but never felt he knew
One unchanged self. Man is himself the god
In this new world, he said to Father's shock.
Its virgin land gave the bold man rebirth
If he would wash his mind of the old faiths,
Cross the wild sea, and live in wilderness.
He thought pure nature molded man to good,
Freed from the old God, His kings and popes.
My father said he was afraid of other men,
And even I, still young, yet saw his dreams
Made a shield. I also saw his loneliness—
The dreaming head cut from our mortal heart.

III

Each single man who hanged him died that year
Through violence, the jurist's *acts of God.*
The town still says he haunts the water oaks.
I went there one night seeking him, but found
Just the pure moonlight falling in between
The moving limbs; quick drops of it hit earth
And ran like mercury on the black, hot ground.
His ghost was wilderness, the burning moon.
Through all these years I wonder if he still
Held to his faith at death. The hanging men
Were just the crude, raw pieces of his god.
When he had landed on these shores, that god
Lived on black slaves and was prepared itself
To spill its godhead's blood in fratricide.
Did he have doubts in those white afternoons
Of that harsh light he had not known at Rome?
The human world will not sustain the weight
Of Heaven and man cannot be God's pure self.
I fear at times, though, that another fate

Claimed him the Sunday morning he was hanged.
The posse was white trash, wild lawless men.
As he was being bound and forced from home,
He could have looked into their faces stained
In grime, the unkempt beards and vicious eyes,
And thought he yet saw god, though evil now
And drunk with wrath against the foreign man.

IV

At first the panic fear she would be killed
Unhinged the woman's mind. It took her time
To grasp the fact that she was safe with us.
But troubles of her mind did not then cease.
There was repressed resentment in the wife
Against her husband who had wrenched her from
Their home and taken her to this raw place
Where Christ could not be found in sacrament.
She feared that she was damned in wilderness
And that her husband's soul now suffered hell.
She changed as she resolved to go back home
And when we reached Mobile—the journey then
Took days and I went too—her soul revived
In the old port, its ships, her hope of home.
Although my father balked, I went with her
Inside her church. A long time she confessed.
When she came from the box I watched and saw
She had some peace and was absolved from sin.
In thickening twilight huge bells were rung.
Before we joined my father, she lingered in
The massive dimness of the church and gazed
As candles burned and lit the altar's gold,
Then crossed herself in tears and turned away.
The next day she embarked and left for Rome.

TOLD FROM THE NINETEENTH CENTURY

A blooming vine covered the side front porch
And hid the woman from the strong full moon.
A bird sang in the new-leaved tulip tree,
But Laura did not heed him that spring night.
She was resolved to face her sister's plight.
The state's asylum loomed as the snake pit
Where Mary would be drugged and left to die.
The sister needed constant care. Last week
She wandered to the outskirts of the town,
Descended cliffs and found the river's brink.
She either jumped or fell. A group of boys
Saved her before the currents sucked her in.
The doctor said it was their father's blood,
Diseased by syphilis, that broke her mind.
Her kin, he judged, could only help her now.
The moon burned white, the Artemis who sheds
The animal's warm blood, bloodless herself.
Laura moved her chair, then faced the light.
She would never conceive. Through her void
She would defeat her father's reckless blood,
Ease it to death, though Mary would die too,
In whose decaying brain his sin lived on.
She could not free her soul from bitterness,
But she could save it from the lawless dead.

THROUGH A GLASS DARKLY

My uncle hated Catholics. Through low guile,
And order that would enslave the gaping mind
He said they grasped at Caesar's naked power.
He hated Jews still more. No law or church
Could hold, for him, the wrath or grace of God
Who voids this world to save the private soul.
But yet he craved tight order. He had made,
Between world wars, the Army his own life
Until his drunken brawls got him discharged.
Back home he studied law, but nothing calmed
That violence in him which made him drink.
He wandered in the streets of our small town
Into all hours, unconscious where he fell.
Whiskey inflamed his swollen face, and tears
Ran out his eyes. I somehow got him home.
He couldn't rest there till I read St. Paul
Out loud beneath a harsh and shadeless bulb,
As if the words alone could make him whole.
"Read *that* again," he shouted from the bed.
But sober he was worse. He turned outward
The rage which he, while drunk, inflicted on
A self he thought was damned. Demonic hate
Built up deep painful pressure in his mind.
I was that rotten thing on whom he wreaked
Its strength, unleasht upon an ungrown boy.
He drove me out. I spent those summer nights
On tent-revivals' sawdust floors and heard
Preachers condemn this sinful world to fire,
As if it had been formed not by their God.

Around midnight I crept back to the house,
Went in the back door my mother had unlocked.
His light was burning in his upstairs room.
Those nights I thought him gone, more alien
When sober than when drunk. He was obese.
I looked up the black stairwell; in my mind
He sat there in the heat with no clothes on—
He was the Buddha of white sagging breasts.
I saw the insects crawling on his screens,
The southern night the hell of his own pain.

THE SLAUGHTER OF THE HERD

The trucks will come tomorrow afternoon.
The herd her family had milked for years
Will then be prodded with electric shocks,
Packed and crammed inside the storied trucks
And driven to the auction ring for slaughter.
Her husband's death had brought her to this pass.
For two hard bitter years she tried alone
To run the dairy. Kindness made her fail—
She lacked the harshness to control rough men.
She knew all this but guilt remained; she felt
In selling she betrayed a binding trust.
Sleep was hopeless. She got up from her bed.
Out on the porch, she looked down toward the woods
Below the house. The pasture stretched between.
The herd, she said, would be somewhere down there.
An urge to see the cows for one last time
In their own nature's world gripped hold of her.
Like someone in a dream, she walked across
The lawn and road, then down the sunken lane.
Night had reached its stillest, deepest hour.
A gibbous moon poured water in the west.
The herd was at the lower pasture where
Dense woods in the night-heat breathed out cool air.
She saw a world not man's in speechless calm.
The cattle as they slept or grazed appeared
Like creatures in some myth, whole and primal.
Their bags hung heavy with the morning milk.
She gazed at them in awe until the scene
Of their approaching death then seized her mind.
She heard the thudding blow against the skull.
A pity for the slaughtered creature dying
Ran through her open soul. She suddenly
Saw her death too, for what was left her now
Her husband dead, the herd dispersed and killed?
She looked up at the sky, the gibbous moon
And saw it as a realm of death and cried.

Aeneas in Modernity

We have no chattel gods to make our home;
We have our psyches where we burn and roam.

OF HARRY DUNCAN, BOOKMAKER

He crafts a print and page that gird
The poem's grace and make it manned.
He creates matter for the word,
The *thisness* of the book in hand,
A poem's flesh, its life conferred.

THE SYMPOSIUM FOR SOCRATES

The polished floor mirrors the burning lamps
Well stocked with oil. We guests are purified.
A slave-boy gives us garlands for our heads.
Balsam is passed around; we scent ourselves
With its perfume. Strong wine is disciplined
Through measured water in the mixing-bowls,
But still it brims and flashes glints of fire
By which our brains, recovering their youth,
Will heat themselves in happiness once more.

*

No flute girls shall seduce us at this feast
And make us stupid in their music's power.
We will not bloat our minds on wildest myths
Concerned with early thugs of made-up gods,
Their brutal loves and broils with savages.
The sometimes bitter, sometimes tragic lore
Of these our human lives, wisdom like salt
Which our own minds can gather from the sea,
Shall be tonight the substance of our talk.